HOMOGRAPHS

bow and bow and other
WORDS THAT LOOK THE SAME
but sound as different as sow and sow

HOMOGRAPHS

Joan Hanson

Published by
Lerner Publications Company
Minneapolis, Minnesota

For Eleanor Johnson

International Standard Book Number: 0-8225-0278-X
Library of Congress Catalog Card Number: 72-1122

Third Printing 1974

hom·o·graph (HAHM-uh-graf) A word that is spelled the same as another word but has a different pronounciation and meaning. These words are homographs: *present* (PREZ-ent)—"a gift"; *present* (pree-ZENT) —"to introduce."

Sow

Sow

Wound

Wound

Object

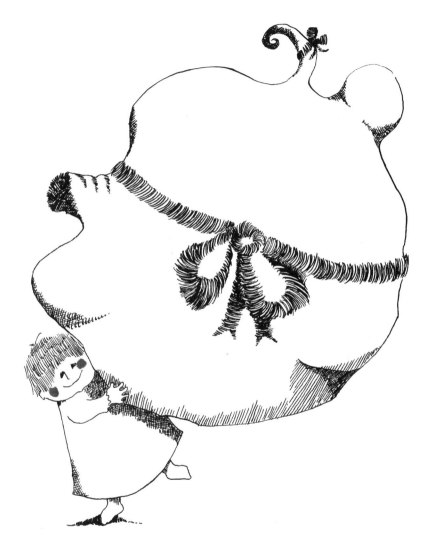

Object

Tear

Tear

Minute

Minute

Bow

Bow

Lead

Lead

Record

Record

Bass

Bass

Dove

Dove

Wind

Wind

Desert

Desert

Refuse

Refuse

BOOKS IN THIS SERIES

ANTONYMS
hot and cold and other
WORDS THAT ARE DIFFERENT
as night and day

MORE ANTONYMS
wild and tame and other
WORDS THAT ARE AS DIFFERENT IN MEANING
as work and play

HOMONYMS
hair and hare and other
WORDS THAT SOUND THE SAME
but look as different as bear and bare

MORE HOMONYMS
steak and stake and other
WORDS THAT SOUND THE SAME
but look as different as chili and chilly

HOMOGRAPHS
bow and bow and other
WORDS THAT LOOK THE SAME
but sound as different as sow and sow

HOMOGRAPHIC HOMOPHONES
fly and fly and other
WORDS THAT LOOK AND SOUND THE SAME
but are as different in meaning as bat and bat

British-American SYNONYMS
french fries and chips and other
WORDS THAT MEAN THE SAME THING
but look and sound
as different as truck and lorry

MORE SYNONYMS
shout and yell and other
WORDS THAT MEAN THE SAME THING
but look and sound
as different as loud and noisy

We specialize in producing quality books for
young people. For a complete list please write

LERNER PUBLICATIONS COMPANY
241 First Avenue North, Minneapolis, Minnesota 55401